ANIMAL TALENT SHOW

A play by Vivian French
Illustrated by Steve Stone

Characters

Ant
(Fantastic Ant)

Bird

Cat

Fantastic Ant: I am Fantastic Ant. I am the judge of the Animal Talent Show!

Cat: He's the best judge ever!

Dog: And he's a big star.

Cow: He's the biggest star ever!

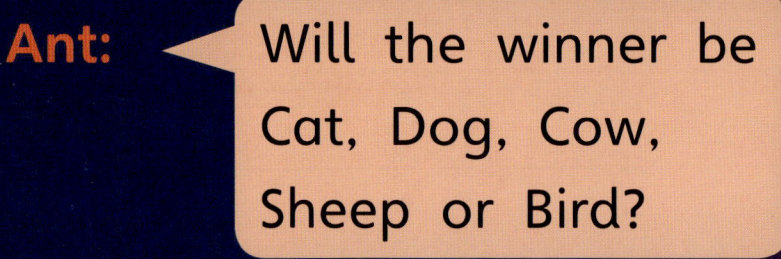

Ant: Will the winner be Cat, Dog, Cow, Sheep or Bird?

Cat: Bird? What bird?

Dog: Bird is late.

Ant: You can start, Cow.

Sheep: Go on then, Cow!

Bird enters.

Bird: Puff, puff! Tweet, tweet! Is this the Animal Talent Show?

Cat: Yes, and you are late!

Bird: I got lost.

Sheep: Sh-sh! It's my go now!

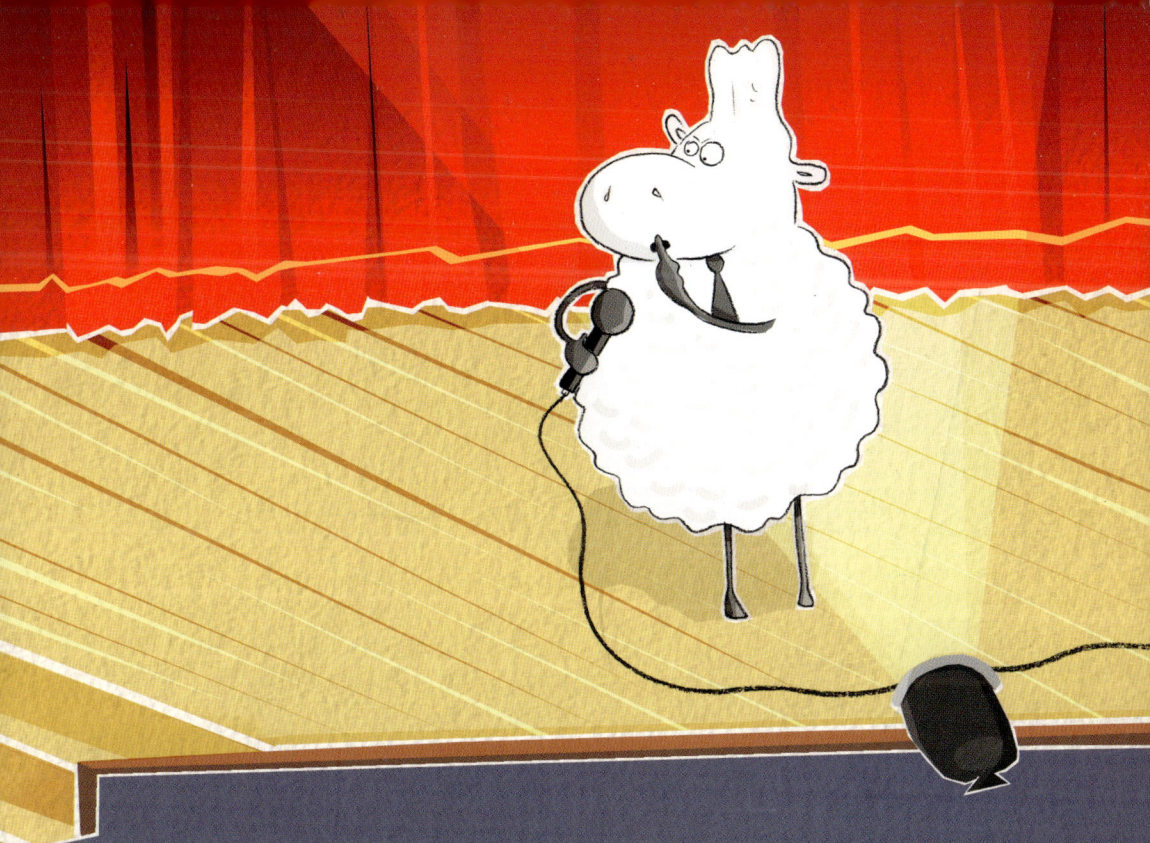

Dog: Be quiet and let Sheep sing.

Sheep: My song is 'The Little Boy Down the Lane'. (*sings*) Baa baa baa! Baa baa **baa**!

Ant: Next!

Cat: It's my turn now! I will sing 'Song to the Queen'. *(sings)* Miaow, miaow, miaow! Miaow, miaow, **miaow!**

Bird: That was a good song!

Dog: No, it was not good. I can sing much better than Cat.

Ant: Next! Your turn, Dog!

Dog: My song is 'The Big Bone Blues'.
(sings) Woof woof woof! Woof woof **woof**!

Bird: That was very good, Dog! You **are** a good singer!

Cow: You go next, Bird.

Bird: But I am too hungry to sing. I need some bird seed!

Cat: Just get on with it!

Bird: Look, a big seed! Yum!

Dog: No! No!

Cow: Stop!

Sheep: Don't do it, Bird!

Ant: HELP!

Bird eats Fantastic Ant.

Bird: That's better. I can sing now! My song is 'Happy, Happy Bird'. *(sings)* Tweet, tweet, tweet!
Tweet, tweet, **tweet**!

Sheep: Stop singing, Bird!

Cat: That was not a seed …